James Augustus Hessey, Church of England, Archdeaconry of Middlesex

Religion Freed from State Control

A charge delivered to the clergy, churchwardens and sidesmen of the

Archdeaconry of Middlesex - at his fifth visitation, at the end of his sixth

year, held at St. Paul's, Covent Garden, May 11th, 1881

James Augustus Hessey, Church of England, Archdeaconry of Middlesex

Religion Freed from State Control
A charge delivered to the clergy, churchwardens and sidesmen of the Archdeaconry of Middlesex - at his fifth visitation, at the end of his sixth year, held at St. Paul's, Covent Garden, May 11th, 1881

ISBN/EAN: 9783337284787

Printed in Europe, USA, Canada, Australia, Japan

Cover: Foto ©Lupo / pixelio.de

More available books at **www.hansebooks.com**

RELIGION (?) FREED FROM STATE CONTROL.

Suct

"Surely in vain the net is spread in the sight of any bird."

A CHARGE

DELIVERED TO THE

Clergy, Churchwardens and Sidesmen

OF THE

ARCHDEACONRY OF MIDDLESEX,

At his Fifth Visitation,

(AT THE END OF HIS SIXTH YEAR),

HELD AT

St. Paul's, Covent Garden, May 11th, 1881,

BY

JAMES AUGUSTUS HESSEY, D.C.L.,

ARCHDEACON OF MIDDLESEX.

LONDON:

THOMAS SCOTT, WARWICK COURT, HOLBORN.

RELIGION (?) FREED FROM STATE CONTROL.

"Surely in vain the net is spread in the sight of any bird."

A CHARGE

DELIVERED TO THE

Clergy, Churchwardens and Sidesmen

OF THE

ARCHDEACONRY OF MIDDLESEX,

At his Fifth Visitation,

(AT THE END OF HIS SIXTH YEAR),

HELD AT

St. Paul's, Covent Garden, May 11th, 1881,

BY

JAMES AUGUSTUS HESSEY, D.C.L.,

ARCHDEACON OF MIDDLESEX.

LONDON:
THOMAS SCOTT, WARWICK COURT, HOLBORN.

1881.

Several passages in the following Charge were shortened in delivery. The documents referred to in the course of it were in many instances summarised, or, with the notes, wholly omitted.

The Archdeacon thanks the Clergy for their full attendance. He has desired a copy of his Charge to be sent to all whose names appear inscribed in his Visitation Book, and to all who have courteously informed him that they were unavoidably kept away.

If any, through miscarriage of Citations, have not been summoned, or, though present, have, by mistake, not inscribed their names in the Book, he will, on hearing from them to either of these effects, desire copies to be sent to them.

MY REVEREND BRETHREN, AND MY BRETHREN THE
CHURCHWARDENS AND SIDESMEN OF THE
ARCHDEACONRY OF MIDDLESEX.

Perhaps, even in this matter-of-fact age, and even on so
solemn an occasion as that of our periodical meeting together,
I may be permitted, not without striking precedents both
from the Old Testament and from the New, to commence
what I have to say with a fiction or allegory. You will
some of you recognise its outline as borrowed from Rogers'
Eclipse of Faith.

On a certain morning a person, on opening his Bible as
usual, found that the familiar leaves presented a perfect
blank. To his great astonishment the holy words had
utterly vanished, and nothing but the white paper remained.
On going abroad and communicating his dismay, he found
that every one was in the same condition with himself—
that their Bibles, of every language, had every syllable
expunged; and more than this, that every book which had
quoted a text from the Bible, presented an hiatus where the
sacred words had been.

This occurrence was greeted as a vast calamity. All felt
that they had lost, either personally, or else for society, what,
though not adequately appreciated, had been a mighty boon.
What should the devout do without their support and stay—
what should the indevout do who, against conscience, had
hitherto not looked into the Bible, but hoped they might have
another opportunity—what should the State do, without such
an aid to its human authority as was provided by the Word
of God?

Lamentation, however, was useless. The only thing to
be done was to endeavour to restore the lost treasure, and

4

to tessellate together such fragments as the memory of individuals could supply. An assembly of divines was forthwith summoned to whom was committed the task of, if it might be, reconstructing the lost document. All possible aid was at their disposal—the jurists who might recall the particulars of the Law—the archæologists who might recall its genealogical and antiquarian matters—the controversialists who might offer their specially favourite texts—the philosophers who might reinstate its moral code—the holy and humble men of heart who had lived on its blessed contents. At length, something like the Original was produced. But it was not *the* Bible. It did not possess its *prestige* or authority. It did not command the general assent of mankind, as the Original had done. And there was so much questioning as to whether, after all, it faithfully replaced the Original, that differences, insignificant before, became magnified into permanent causes of disunion—in fact "the old was emphatically better."

Viewed, no doubt, as a possible event, the imagination of this story is an extravagant one. But so was that displayed in Jotham's parable of the trees "going forth on a time to anoint a king over them"—in which speech is attributed respectively to the olive-tree, the fig-tree, and the vine, and not merely speech, but destructive intentions, to the energetic bramble. There, as here, the occurrences supposed could not have taken place without an alteration of what we term the ordinary conditions of nature. But that which I have adduced may serve the purpose of an allegory to point the following moral. That gifts, not sufficiently valued may be withdrawn, suddenly and unexpectedly, that universal regret may be experienced on the discovery, by the late possessors,

"Nil sibi legatum, præter plorare, suisque."
Hor: *Sat.* II. 5, 69.

and that this regret will exhibit itself in an attempt, which,

after all, must be but partially successful, to replace what
has been carelessly or indolently forfeited.

But for the interpretation of all this. We are threatened,
and threatened, so confident are our assailants, speedily, not
indeed with an evisceration of our Bibles, and the erasure
of their golden words, but with the subversion, so far as man
can subvert it, of what has been for fifteen hundred years, at
the very least, established as the witness and keeper of
Holy Writ amongst us. A society has been for some time
set on foot with a title as ingenious as it is disingenuous—it
is called a society *not* for destroying religion—far from it—
but a society for the "Liberation of Religion from State
Patronage and Control." Could anything be kinder or more
considerate than an endeavour to strike off the fetters with
which Religion is needlessly encumbered? But wait a little,
and I will tell you how the movement began and how it has
taken its present form. In April 1844, an Anti-State-
Church Conference was held by certain Nonconformists;
and in that year was formed what in effect was the Liberation Society, under the title of "The British Anti-State
Church Association." For nine years it retained that somewhat startling designation. But bye and bye it was dis-
covered to be too startling for the purpose, and a less
transparently aggressive policy seemed preferable. At a
Conference held in 1853, the Executive Committee reported
as follows: "In suggesting a change in the name of this
Association, we have deferred to the feeling expressed in
many quarters that its present designation is liable to mis-
apprehension, is needlessly offensive, and is in other respects
undesirable." The name was accordingly changed into that
of "The Society for the Liberation of Religion from State
Patronage and Control." Well, simple people, who know
nothing of this little bit of history, are forsooth to imagine
that it is a combination of devout and serious men, vexed in
their very hearts at the secular bonds which shackle the

energies of the earnest, and determined to bring back the Church to what they consider a more apostolical condition. Here and there amongst its supporters some such men may perhaps be found. There may be a few religious Nonconformists, animated with the spirit of Puritan ancestors. There may be a few Churchmen, harassed with the Public Worship Regulation Act, impatient of legal control generally, and fondly imagining that a freedom of doctrine and ritual will be allowed them under a new state of things, which they conceive themselves to be denied at present. But both of these classes, granting for the moment that they exist, should be reminded of these important points—that there is scarcely a Nonconformist sect, how insignificant soever, that does not now possess at least Chapel property*—that such property is usually held on Trust that certain doctrines shall be preached therein—that if a Minister is displaced on the ground of his not teaching such doctrines, a Court of Law must be appealed to—and that thus the tenets of the sect must come under secular arbitrament. A vast induction of cases† might be cited in support of these assertions,

---

* It is not generally known, but is set forth in a Return to the House of Commons, on the Motion of Mr. Cubitt, M.P., ordered May 8, 1873, and ordered to be printed, July 10, 1873, how many these Nonconformist Endowments are. That Return gives a " List of the Orders which, during the Ten Years ending on the 31st day of March, 1873, have been made by the Charity Commissioners appointing Trustees or establishing Schemes for Nonconformist Chapels or Institutions, or their Endowments, distinguishing the Dates, Name or Designation of the Chapel or Institution, and the General Objects of the Order in each Case." The number of Orders in the List is 854. But in addition to those included in it, the following numbers of Orders relating to Nonconformist Chapels or Institutions, or their Endowments, but not coming strictly within the terms mentioned in the Order of the House, have been made by the Commissioners within the period specified in that Order, viz. :—

Authorising Sales	84
Authorising Leases	93
Authorising Transfer of Stock to the Official Trustees ...	133
Miscellaneous	113
	423

† See a List extending from 1840 to 1869, in Appendix C., to Speech of Mr. George Cubitt, M.P., July 2, 1872. Published by Ch. Def. Instit., 1871.

but it may be enough to mention three. One of them is the celebrated case of Lady Hewley's Charity, which consists of large endowments for *Orthodox Dissenters*. A question arose, What are Orthodox Dissenters, and do Unitarians come under that denomination? It was decided, in 1842, after much litigation, that they did not. Temporal as the Court appealed to—that of Chancery—undoubtedly was, discussions on the most spiritual topics, the Divinity of our Saviour, and the like, formed necessarily part of the proceedings.

The second case shall be given in the words of Sir Roundell Palmer, now Lord Selborne. He spoke thus:* "It has been my lot to be concerned professionally in settling the differences of a voluntary religious body—the respectable body of Congregationalists, commonly called Baptists—upon what one might presume to be a rather critical point of their system—namely, whether or not baptism was necessary to justify a Baptist Minister in treating a person as a communicant; and the Court of Chancery decided that it was not. I believe the Court decided, in a manner which has been acquiesced in ever since, that baptism is not indispensable among the Baptists. I do not in the least degree mean to imply anything theological; it would be most unbecoming in me to do so; what I mean is, that among Nonconformists, as in the Church of England, there are different parties, some thinking one thing and some another; they do not agree as to whether a particular thing is necessary or right to be done or held by the Minister. And then the question arises, whether the Minister, differing from some of his Congregation on a given point, has a right to hold the pulpit and continue his ministration in that Church; accordingly they come to the Court of Chancery to decide that question; and so should we have to act if we were disestablished now. Let no man delude himself with the idea that, as long as men are citizens of the State, and carry on the services of religion by the use of temporal means, they can escape from the obligation of being governed by the laws of the land. The laws of the land cannot impose upon any persons the necessity of believing one doctrine or the other; if the law of the land rules questions, in which they as members of a particular Church are concerned, contrary to their consciences, they, of course, may either acquiesce or leave that Church; but they never can by any possibility escape from the necessity of submitting to some control on the part of the law. And, with reference to those Clergy who have been made uneasy because uniformity of ritual is enforced in a sense in which they did not expect, or in a manner more strict than they expected, I cannot but think that the great majority of them will agree, that the principle of obedience to law is of infinitely greater importance than any disputed form of ritual whatever; and, at all events, they must see, that points of that sort, when disputed, must go for interpretation to the law. Certainly it ought to be understood, that they cannot obtain absolute independence of the Civil Courts by means of Disestablishment; and for my own part I think the effect of Disestablishment would be that most points in controversy would be ruled more strictly against minorities by the Legislative Assembly of a Disestablished Church, than, as a general rule, they are likely to be by the Courts of Law."

The third case is one which has been recently decided—that of Jones v. Stannard, in the Court of Vice-Chancellor Hall. Mr. Stannard was the Pastor of the Ramsden Street Chapel in the Town of Huddersfield, which belongs to the "Protestant Dissenters of the Congregational denomination, otherwise called Independents, being Pædo-Baptists."

The trustees of this chapel were twenty-one persons, who held the property under the provisions of a certain trust-deed, and who were bound "to permit only such persons to officiate in the said chapel and premises" as held "the doctrines specified in the schedule of this deed." This schedule contained clauses which plainly enunciated the doctrines commonly called Calvinistical, including those of the total depravity of man, absolute predestination, &c. Mr. Stannard had been appointed to the charge of it, but, after his appointment, demanded a liberty of interpreting the doctrines of the sect, which the trustees considered to be incompatible with the retention of his office. Resign he would not. He had interpreted the terms of the trust, or in other words, " the articles of the sect," according to his conscience. So, the matter was brought into Court, and after a long and elaborate argument had been heard from Counsel on both sides, and " experts" belonging to the denomination had been examined and cross-examined in due form, the Vice-Chancellor decreed that Mr. Stannard's teaching had not been in accordance with the doctrines laid down in the trust-deed, and accordingly gave judgment against him. In others words, the Civil Court ruled that Mr. Stannard must relinquish his office of Pastor of the Ramsden Street Chapel, giving him the usual opportunity of appealing to a higher Court if he thought proper to do so. If Mr. Stannard had persisted, in spite of this admonition of the Court, in officiating in the chapel, he would have been guilty of contempt, and the Court would have proceeded to enforce its judgment, in which case he would have been conveyed to prison. " We believe," says a writer,* from whose comment on the case I have extracted the above statement, " he has chosen a less heroic course, and that, with the majority of the congregation who agree with him, he will secede from the whole body, and with his followers set up a chapel of his own, in which he will teach the doctrines he holds to the full." This, however, is not the question. The real question is, will Disestablishment give unlimited freedom, or even a freedom which an Established Church enjoys? If after these proofs any persons are sanguine

---

* In *The National Church*, March, 1881, p. 61.

enough to believe this, all we can say to them is, what the
Athenians said to the Melians,* μακαρίσαντες ὑμῶν τὸ
ἀπειρόκακον οὐ ζηλοῦμεν τὸ ἄφρον. Try other expedients for
relief, if you can find such. Pray for the repeal of certain
Acts, or the rehabilitation of certain Courts† or the like, but
do not resort to a remedy which may, and indeed must, prove
worse than the disease.

Of this by the way. I return to what is indeed an
ungracious task but still is a very necessary one—the exposure
of what are the designs of the so-called " Society for the
Liberation of Religion from State Patronage and Control"—
and of the methods by which it is endeavouring to compass
those designs. It will follow to give you what hints I may
for countermining, while there is yet time, the efforts of its
insidious warfare.

Before, however, I do this, I would say a word upon what
are likely to be the results of its operations, if successful, so
far as those results can be gathered from the tendencies of
the operations, and from the published sentiments of some
who are assisting in them. I fear very much that they will be
most thoroughly injurious to the cause of true Religion in this
country. I do not indeed, for one moment, mean that every
one who has joined it places such a result consciously or
distinctly before him as an object to be attained. There are,
as I have said already, " deceived as well as deceivers in its
ranks"—ignorant persons as well as persons who know
perfectly what they are about. Enthusiasts, dissatisfied with

---

* Thuc. : v. 106.

† It may be hoped that something will be done in this direction in
accordance with the Resolution carried in the House of Lords, on March 8,
1881, on the motion of the Archbishop of Canterbury, viz. :—" That an humble
address be presented to Her Majesty, praying that Her Majesty will be pleased
to appoint a Royal Commission to inquire into the constitution and working of
the Ecclesiastical Courts as created or modified under the Reformation Statutes
of the 24th and 25th years of King Henry the Eighth, and any subsequent
Acts."

the present state of things and, like the Fifth Monarchy men
described by Scott in his *Peveril of the Peak*, combining with
men of a very different character.*

One is reminded of the words of the Greek Poet :—

ξυνώμοσαν γὰρ, ὄντες ἔχθιστοι τὸ πρίν,
πῦρ καὶ θάλασσα, καὶ τὰ πίστ᾽ ἐδειξάτην
φθείροντε τὸν δύστηνον Ἀργείων στρατόν.
Æsch. : *Agam*. 633—635.

But, with every charitable allowance, it is impossible to
blind ourselves to the fact that on the list of its Executive
Committee is to be found the name of Mr. John Morley, the
editor of " The Life of Diderot," which has been recently—
October, 1880—the subject of an article in the *Quarterly
Review*. Now Diderot was not merely a disbeliever in
Churches, or in Revealed Religion, but even in Natural
Religion. One of his sayings was, " It is important not to
take hemlock for parsley, but not important at all to believe
or disbelieve in God,"† Another was : " We must put
theology to the sword." It might have been hoped that
the editor of his Life would have disclaimed sympathy
with such statements, but here is what the *Quarterly Review*
says of him, not ignoring his talents (no candid mind could
do that), but deploring their application : " To listen to
Mr. Morley, when he speaks as an historian and a critic,
is always a pleasure, and were he content with instructing
us out of his abundant stores of information, we should

---

* " As to this which lies before us," said Christian, " my brother Bridgenorth brings to it the simplicity, though not the harmlessness of the dove,
and I the subtlety of the serpent. He hath the leading of the saints who
are moved by the Spirit ; and I can add to their efforts a powerful body,
who have for their instigators, the world, the devil, and the flesh."

" And can you," said Julian, looking at Bridgenorth, " accede to such an
unworthy union ?"

" I unite not with them," said Bridgenorth ; " but I may not without guilt
reject the aid which Providence sends to assist His servants. We are
ourselves few, though determined. Those whose swords come to help the
cutting down of the harvest, must be welcome. When their work is
wrought, they will be converted or scattered."—*Peveril of the Peak*, chap. 43.

† See *The National Church*, January, 1881.

receive his teaching with unmixed gratitude. But he will not be satisfied without showing himself as something else at the same time; and that is, an open, resolute propagandist of what may be styled Philosophical Atheism. His position towards the most majestic and venerable of human beliefs is not a matter of doubtful inference from a passage here or there, or from an under-current of thought flowing obscurely beneath the surface of his narrative or his discussions; he poses before us almost defiantly in the character of a determined and unflinching opponent of Theism, and will not allow us for a moment to lose sight of his attitude." Here also is another fact. Mr. Frederic Harrison, whose views as a " Positivist" are well known, delivered a lecture on Church and State at Manchester and Liverpool, which after having appeared in the *Fortnightly Review* (of which Mr. John Morley is the editor), was published in a substantive form by the Society.

To this it may be added that Dr. Allon, a Congregationalist of Islington, having assumed that the existence of a National Church is an infringement of civil rights, said, in a speech at a Public Meeting of the Liberation Society, held June, 1880, " We have been found fighting side by side with the Roman Catholic, and side by side with the Jew; and I for one am prepared to fight side by side with the Infidel and the Atheist, in all questions that compromise their civil rights as citizens." One seems to be listening to those strange aspirations in the *Critic:*—

> " Behold thy votaries submissive beg,
> That thou wilt deign to grant them *all* they ask ;
> Assist them to accomplish *all* their ends,
> And *sanctify whatever means* they use
> To gain them !"

I confess that, even if I knew nothing more about the matter than is to be gathered from these facts, I should be inclined to look suspiciously upon an alliance thus unscrupulously entered into. But, passing over any inferences

which might be drawn from the motley character of the
confederacy, I go on to observe that the avowed objects
proposed are the Disestablishment and Disendowment of the
Church of England, which is the main prop of Religion in
the Land. Among other reasons, no doubt, some of them
dislike it, as a standing evidence that the State has a conscience—a feeling of duty which causes it to connect the
conduct of men, its subjects, in this world, with their destinies
in that other. A troublesome companion that State-con-
science which the Society has discarded—an inconvenient
matter of thought that other world, which some of its
supporters have done their best to ignore. The Disestablishment is not to be gradual—men are not to be
allowed to wean themselves gradually from their ancient
belief and their most cherished associations. A time is
to be fixed, and then, as suddenly and sharply as
our apologue supposed the contents of the Bible to be
obliterated, Churchmen who have been indulging in fancied
security, or wasting their energies in differences upon smaller
points, or agreeing to fraternise with persons they disagree
with, upon social questions as they are called, are to wake up
and find that they are disestablished. There can be no
mistake whatever upon this point. A deliberate scheme
has been put forth by this Society, the work of a Special
Committee which has spent two years in its preparation.
The 3rd Section of this document asserts it in so many words,
and speciously adds that it proposes this suddenness of
execution out of benevolent considerations to the Church.
" The members of the Disestablished Church would suffer,
(it tenderly says), the great disadvantage of having to work
under a double system; being disestablished in some Parishes,
and established in others. This would make the re-organisation
of the Church impossible, and would lead to confusion which
would be embarrassing to the State, and absolutely ruinous
to the Church." And in Sect. 9 it is suggested that the

dismissal of the Clergy should be complete and thorough; that they should not, as in Ireland, have imposed upon them continued performance of their duties, as a condition of receiving compensation from the State — (*observe the assumption that Church property is State property*). This is to be reversed in England. At a certain date to be fixed by Act of Disestablishment, "all the holders of ecclesiastical office in the Establishment are to be released from obligation to the State (*observe this again*) to discharge their present duties. Glebe Houses and Parsonages become forthwith the property of the State—and though it is professed that their occupants are not to be inconveniently hurried, and we are not to realise the words of the Poet immediately,—

> "Pellitur paternos
> In sinu ferens Deos,
> Et uxor et vir sordidosque natos."

they are only there on sufferance. They have nothing to do with, and can do nothing in, the holy places wherein they used to minister—Cathedral and Parochial Churches alike are to be taken in hand by the State. The ministrations of Fifteen Hundred years are to be brought to an end. Whatever surplus remains, after settlement of all specified claims, is to be devoted " to education—to the maintenance of the poor—to effecting great sanitary improvements—to the reduction of the National Debt, or to other objects of a *secular**

---

* It would seem that the word *Secular* is introduced, among other reasons, in order to disclaim any intention on the part of those promoting the Liberation movement to share in the revenues of the Church when Disestablished and Disendowed. In Ireland, however, £755,816 have been taken out of the revenues of the Irish Church to form a Capital for the Presbyterian *Regium Donum*, and £372,331 to form a Capital for the endowment of *Maynooth*, and the Government has thus saved the interest of a Capital of £1,128,147. It may be surmised that many of the sects who are joining in the cry against the English Church would scarcely be more disinterested if a portion of its spoil were offered to them. They have many endowments already, and they might say, why should we not increase them? And as we have seen, they are, so far as endowments go, exactly under the same liability to State control that the Church is. To be consistent then, they will be obliged to admit that Religion is shackled among themselves, and ought to be anxious to be disendowed.

character, (*observe* religious *is carefully excluded*) which would be beneficial to the whole nation." (Sect. 28.)

With merely the outline of a project so monstrous in view, well might Mr. Gladstone declare (as he has more than once done,) that " Disestablishment does not come within the range of practical Politics," and say, as he said in the House of Commons, May 16, 1873, " The Church of England has not only been a part of the history of this country, but a part so vital, entering so profoundly into the entire life and action of the country, that the severing of the two would leave nothing behind but a bleeding and lacerated mass. Take the Church of England out of the History of England, and the History of England becomes a chaos without order, without life, and without meaning." To these words I would add that the Church of England, as an establishment, is so completely an element of our social system, so connected with our best sympathies, with our families, with our institutions of every kind, and with the arrangements of property through the length and breadth of the land, that not merely the History of England, but the very character of England would be affected by its disappearance.

This, however, brings me to notice that Disestablishment is to be accompanied by Disendowment. With a few exceptions, which are obviously introduced in order to present a colourable semblance of equitable consideration—the Clergy are to be divested of their freeholds—and if they are to receive compensation, it is on the utterly false assumption that they have been " public officials," and are to be dealt with as " other public officials whose services are no longer required by the State." I call this an utterly false assumption—*First*, because the oldest Church Property was not originally given by the State, but bestowed, whether in the shape of Tithes, or of Estates, or of Churches, or of Parsonages, by the piety of individual proprietors. *Secondly*, because, with the exception of the One Million and a Half, granted for Church Building in the second and third decades of this century, nothing whatever has been given by the State at any time, in the way of money. *Thirdly*, because what the State has done has been to guarantee the Clergy the possession of their Property and of the Income derived therefrom, on the due performance of their duties. It has interfered, indeed, thrice. Once at the Reformation, but then it took away arbitrarily and gave nothing. Once again, at the establishment of the Ecclesiastical Commission, but then it merely set on foot a machinery, so to re-distribute property, as to provide that the duties of the Clergy should be more efficiently performed. And once again, when the Tithe Commutation Act was passed. This, however, was not an Act to legalize the payment of Tithes for the first time. They had from time immemorial been a charge on the produce of the land, and had always been recoverable by process of law. Its object was simply this. Whereas Tithes had hitherto been paid in kind, and such payment had occasionally given rise to misunderstandings between the tithe-payer and the tithe-receiver—henceforth, a payment should be made in money, and called not Tithe, but Tithe Rent-Charge.* *Fourthly*, because, though it has been

---

* It is worth noticing that, though it was not intended that such should be the case, the tithe-receiver has been greatly disadvantaged by the arrangement made by the Tithe Commutation Act. The intention of that Act was to strike a fair bargain between the tithe-receivers (or tithe-owners) and the tithe-payers, that is the land-owners, whose property was subject to tithes. This may be thus illustrated:—The annual value of tithes to the tithe-receivers in 1836 was four millions sterling, the annual value of titheable property was thirty-three millions. The most valuable element in tithe property was that it increased with the improvement of titheable land. Since the year 1835 to the year 1876, we have the authority of Mr. Caird (*The Landed Interest*, p. 131, 1879) for asserting that titheable property has increased from thirty-three to fifty-four millions; meanwhile the rent-charge of the tithe-receivers has remained stationary. The result, as I have said, was not anticipated by either of the parties to the bargain. But the fact remains that the tithe-receivers have surrendered to the land-owners or tithe-payers about two millions a year, which would have been theirs but for the Tithe Commutation Act. But for that Act, tithe would be now six millions a year, instead of a commuted rent-charge of about four millions. A similar

shown by a recent Parliamentary Return that 2,581 separate Incumbencies or Parochial Districts have been created by the Ecclesiastical Commission or Church Building Commission since 1842, the money for this has been derived from Church Funds aided by contributions of individual Churchmen. To this should be added two other facts: 1. That a return made some short time ago, at the instance of Lord Hampton, places the sum which has been raised by Members of the Church for Church Building and Church Restoration, since 1840, at the enormous figure of 25½ millions. (Even this does not include Restorations which cost less than £500.) 2. As a specimen of what is still going on, that in one year, 1880, in one Archdeaconry alone, that of Lewes, £96,071 were laid out in Church Building, Restoration and Endowment—a small fraction of this being from re-distributed Church Funds, the rest contributed by Congregations and Individuals. *Fifthly*, because the exceptions allowed are allowed upon the very grounds on which we refuse to grant the equity of confiscating the older endowments, namely the voluntary as opposed to the State character of their foundation.

How the *programme* above indicated is to be carried out we shall see presently. Supposing, however, for a moment that it were carried out, would it be easy to reconstruct the Ecclesiastical Edifice thus rudely and ruthlessly thrown down? The prospects of the Disestablished Irish Church

---

disadvantage to many of the tithe-receivers in the City of London was caused by the Fire Act, which substituted a fixed money payment for tithes.

The following Table will show how the existing Tithe Rent-charge is distributed. It is taken from a Return ordered by the House of Commons in 1856:—

Total Rent-charges payable to

Clerical Appropriators and Lessees	...	£678,345	11 1¾
Parochial Incumbents	... ...	2,410,506	7 6¼
Lay Impropriators	... ...	765,427	5 4¾
Schools, Colleges, &c.	... ...	195,948	5 11¼

£4,050,227 10 0¼

B

are not encouraging. Though large sums have been raised towards the formation of a Capital, these are utterly inadequate to the purpose of maintaining with the strictest economy even the Parochial Clergy. The embarrassment of Landed Proprietors in Ireland is so great that in many cases they have been obliged to retract their promises of an annual Parochial cess in aid of the interest of that Capital. And it is to be feared that as the Confiscation of Tithes in Lay hands will accompany the Confiscation of Tithes in Clerical hands—and as the title to all property is endangered when one class of property has been successfully assailed—efforts at reconstruction, however earnest, will fail of results even financially and materially. Mr. Harrison, indeed, treats this question very summarily. He says, " It will be a lasting disgrace to the members of it (the Disestablished Church), if they suffer it to perish ; if they do nothing to maintain its discipline, its organisation, its ritual; if they suffer its historical memorials to drop out of its hand, its Congregations to disperse, and its parishes to be without a Minister to teach them." But he seems to have forgotten that the members of the Church may prefer retaining the advantages they already possess, to allowing them to slip from their hands first, and being taunted with disgraceful inactivity if they do not regain them. If we desire any further illustration of this, we have only to look at what is now going on in Oxford and Cambridge. The chief satisfactory guarantees for the religious instruction of Students in the principles of the Church of England in the ancient Colleges have been recently swept away. A partial endeavour is being made to supply the want by the erection of new Colleges, as Keble College in Oxford, and Selwyn College in Cambridge, and other institutions of a more limited character. But what are these compared with the advantages which we have inconsiderately allowed to be forfeited? The Anti-Church movement is now going further still in these venerable places of education, formerly the strongholds of the Church. In accordance with the wishes of one generation of Fellows, the Clerical Fellowships in each College are being reduced to a *minimum*—the natural desire of parents to the contrary being utterly neglected, or, at least, not being consulted. They remonstrate, but are not listened to. Here remedy is impossible. Then let us look at a similar case. The Scholarships at the Universities which might have been available for poor Students seeking Holy Orders have been in almost every case thrown open to unlimited competition, and are now frequently enjoyed by persons whose circumstances have enabled them to command means of superior training. The Church is obliged, as well as she can, but after all, most inadequately, to educate men for the Ministry, by such Societies as the Ordination Candidates' Exhibition Fund, the *Scholae Cancellarii* at Lincoln and the like.

These are some of the results of our not having been wise in time.

It may also be questioned whether the Church, supposing it to be disestablished, can ever be that comprehensive, liberal, body which it is now—whether it will not split up into sects—or whether, if professing to be one, it will not be with a creed either bigotedly narrowed, or else extended in a Latitudinarian direction. Lord Macaulay remarks, in regard to the Nonjuring Communion, "That Little Church, without Temples, revenues or dignities, was even more distracted by internal disputes than the Great Church which retained possession of Cathedrals, Tithes, and Peerages."

Prevention, however, is at all times better than cure. Even if the cure could be more complete than we can imagine, the *prestige* of the Church could never be restored.

How then may such a catastrophe be prevented? I said to you last year that I have not the slightest fear, (so long as she is true to herself,) for the interests of the Church even as an Establishment. And you will remember that I also stated that such men as Mr. Gladstone, the Marquis of Hartington, Lord Selborne, and Mr. W. E. Forster, if any faith is to be reposed on their solemn public declarations or public acts, are not men to be feared. To these may be added another Member of the present Government, Sir William Harcourt, the Home Secretary. He declared, speaking at Oxford, on December 21, 1874, " In my opinion, he is a purblind politician who does not perceive that the residuary legatee of Disestablishment will infallibly be the Church of Rome." I said also that, " No Statesman wantonly assails or tears to pieces an Institution, the growth of centuries, to which he is personally attached, or which he cannot help confessing to be doing incalculable good." I hold to my deliberately expressed opinion. But then these eminent men must be supported against the extreme persons who are to be found among their adherents, by the Church being true to herself. So the inquiry arises, "When is the Church true to herself?" One and the highest way of her being so, is when Clergy and Laity, in their several positions, as I trust and believe is the case with you, my Brethren, labour for the glory of God. The Clergy being diligent in their ministrations, the Laity seconding their efforts, and both personally profiting by them, and deepening and widening the soil over which the Divine influence extends or should extend. It is, however, still a part of their duty, while engaged in the work of saving their own souls and the souls of those about them, to provide also " *ne quid Respublica detrimenti capiat* "—that is, to look to the outworks of the General Body, the Church ; to defend it from attacks ; and if such attacks have become organised and systematic, to enter upon organised and systematic Church Defence. Days may arise, and often do arise, when apart from the selfishness of isolation, it is to the highest degree imprudent " to fight for one's own hand"—

that is, without combination. And no one has a right to plead that he is so occupied with his immediate concerns as to be exempt from the duty of corporate action. The Jews in Nehemiah's time, " which builded on the wall, and they that bare burdens, with those that laded, every one with one of his hands wrought in the work, and with the other hand held a weapon." They were personally on their guard, but they were not therefore without combination, for Nehemiah said, " The work is great and large, and we are separated upon the wall, one far from another. In what place, therefore, ye hear the sound of the trumpet, resort ye thither unto us : our God shall fight for us." (*Nehemiah* iv. 17-20.) Those Jews may give us a hint. Let us not be afraid of being thought afraid, and so intermit preparations for defence, when danger is nigh. Let us not fear the adage *qui s'excuse s'accuse*, and so refuse to meet assertions which we know are being made about us, and which are misleading many, and must mislead more, unless they are confuted. It may be, in the abstract, a noble thing, to imitate those aged Roman Senators, who, are thus described by Livy : " *Turba seniorum, domos regressa, adventum hostium obstinato ad mortem animo expectabat. Qui eorum curules gesserant magistratus, ut in fortunae pristinae honorumque aut virtutis insignibus morerentur, quae augustissima vestis est tensas ducentibus triumphantibusve, ea vestiti medio aedium eburneis sellis sedere.*" (LIV: v. 41.) Thus persons have said, Let the storm of Disestablishment come, it will find us doing our duty—our Clergy performing their functions, the Laity worshipping—" *Impavidos ferient ruinae.*" This is all very well. But when did those whom Livy describes assume this passive attitude for themselves, and who were they who thus assumed it ? They posed thus, " *Satis jam omnibus, ut in tali re, ad arcem tuendam compositis.*" And they were men who, though they had heretofore acted for their country, were now in extreme old age, and unable to do more than

counsel. Such counsel as they could give they gave. Shall
we, who are in our vigour, have done our duty by mere
passive resistance? If there is any one who thinks so, let
him ponder the words of the Archbishop of Canterbury at a
recent important Meeting held at Lambeth.* The Archbishop
said, in his opening remarks, that "it was indeed true and
had long been the prevalent opinion, that the quiet pursuance
of their duties by the Clergy and other members of the
Church, without troubling themselves about external assaults,
was the best position in which to appear before the world."
But that "the persistent aggressive policy and misrepre-
sentations of the Church's enemies rendered it impossible to
sit perfectly quiet, or refrain from measures for dispelling
ignorance, and repelling attacks." The same tone was
adopted by other speakers, and I remember having been
particularly struck with what was said by a Layman.

His language was somewhat as follows : " The Clergy,
if they desire to effect any real influence over the national

---

* This was a private Conference of persons interested in the work of the
Church Defence Institution, held at Lambeth Palace on March 28, 1881,
under the presidency of the Archbishop of Canterbury. Amongst those
present were the Marquis of Salisbury, K.G., the Earls of Redesdale and
Dartmouth, the Bishop of Chichester, Lord Clinton, Lord O'Neill, Lord
Henry Scott, M.P., Right Hon. Sir Richard Cross, M.P., the Hon.
W. Egerton, M.P., Lieut.-Col. Hon. G. Windsor Clive, M.P., Sir Hardinge
Giffard, M.P., J. G. Talbot, Esq., M.P., H. Birley, Esq., M.P., J. Round,
Esq., M.P., Right Hon. H. Cecil Raikes, Sir Richard Wilbraham, K.C.B.,
Sir E. Hertslet, C.B., Dr. Tristram, Q.C., the Dean of Wells (Mr. Johnson);
the Archdeacon of Middlesex (Dr. Hessey) ; the Archdeacon of Ely
(Mr. Emery) W. U. Heygate, J. Richardson, Sydney Gedge, H. G. Hoare,
W. Hoare, F. A. White, J. B. White, J. F. Burnaby Atkins, G. B. Hughes,
H. D. Davenport, Esqrs.; Capt. Field, R.N., Revs. Capel Cure, Dr. Alfred
T. Lee, Randall T. Davidson, H. G. Dickson, and S. Thackrah. Letters of
apology were read from the Archbishop of York, the Bishops of London,
Durham, Lincoln, Gloucester and Bristol, Ely, Truro, and Liverpool, the
Earls of Devon, Stanhope, and Powis, Lord Penrhyn, Lord Charles Bruce,
M.P., the Right Hon. W. H. Smith, M.P., the Right Hon. Spencer H. Walpole,
M.P., Sir William Rose, Sir J. Kennaway, Bart., M.P., Sir J. McGarel Hogg,
Bart., M.P., Sir J. R. Mowbray, Bart., M.P., the Vice-Chancellor of the
University of Cambridge (Dr. E. H. Perowne), the Hon. and the Rev. E. Carr
Glyn, and Rev. Canon G. H. Wilkinson.

counsels in the future, must not disdain the weapons which the development of our Institutions, and which, therefore, we may say, without irreverence, the decree of Providence has placed within their hands. No doubt it is a far more congenial, agreeable, and dignified position to stand aside from the contest altogether. They may take the view that it is for others to decide whether the Church shall stand or fall, and that they will remain passive and receive the blow which is to come; but do not let them think that they can combine two opposite advantages. They may have the dignity of this kind of martyrdom if they remain still. They may save the Church if they will stir. But they cannot both save the Church and have the agreeable incidents of the position and the attitude which so many of them prefer. The crisis is thickening—the moment for such delicacies has passed, and those who are earnest to save the Church of England must not disdain to fight for her.''

The immediate effects of this language and of other speeches of a similar character, were,

First, that the Resolutions following were carried unanimously:

1. " That in view of the strenuous and persistent efforts now being made to prejudice the public mind against the National Church, it is indispensable that a corresponding effort be made on the part of all attached Churchmen, without distinction of religious or political party, to take such steps as may be needful for putting distinctly before the country the truth as regards the work, history, and position of the Church of England.''

2. " That in order to carry the above Resolution into effect, it is necessary to make an immediate and substantial addition to the funds of the Church Defence Institution, and that his Grace the Archbishop of Canterbury be requested to commend the matter to the serious attention of the Clergy and Laity of the Church.''

Secondly, that the Archbishop intimated his intention to issue a Pastoral on the subject.

Thirdly, that a considerable sum was promised in the Room for the purpose of strengthening the hands of the Church Defence Institution.

I trust, my Brethren, that we shall see our way to prevent these Resolutions from being a mere dead letter.

Meanwhile, let us examine more nearly, What the Promoters of Disestablishment are doing—that is, by what means they are striving to attain their object? And then, by what means we should counteract their operations. They boast that they have the will, and only want the power, which they are determined to gain, of destruction. We humbly think that, with God's aid, we have the power to resist them—let us gird ourselves, like men, to the will!

It appears from the published documents of the Liberation Society,

1. That its promoters subscribed a sum of about £100,000, and that it professes to have an income of £14,000 a year.*

2. That the administration of its funds is in the hands of a Central Committee in London, which has divided the whole of England into districts for the purpose of carrying on agitation against the Church.

3. That each of these districts has salaried Superintendents, with a large body of agitators at their disposal.

4. That these agitators are abundantly supplied with literature upon the subject of Disestablishment. And that they not merely disseminate it in the form of leaflets and pamphlets, but hold meetings and lectures regularly or occasionally, year after year, and even month after month, in various towns and villages up and down the country.

5. That in every County, as well as in important

---

* I observed in the *Times* of yesterday that a Legacy of £2,500 was bequeathed by a gentleman, named Courtauld, to "The Society for the Liberation of Religion from State Patronage and Control."

Boroughs and large Villages, there are subordinate Committees in connection with that in London—and that there are intermediately local centres by which the connection is actively sustained.

6. That, wherever [it is possible, attempts are made to enlist local newspapers in favour of the movement, and that no effort is spared to interest men of the most diverse religious views, or of anti-religious views, in the cause of Liberationism.

7. That Liberationism is studiously confounded with Liberalism, as if the Church were confined to one political party, and as if even advanced Liberals such as the Duke of Devonshire and Lord Hatherley were not among the greatest supporters of the Church.

8. That the Ministers and the periodicals of various Noncomformist bodies are in many instances in active alliance with the Liberation Society and pushing forward its work.*

9. That not merely is the literature put forth enormous in amount, or the lectures delivered numerous, (we are informed that in the year 1879 the Liberation Society circulated 3,141,767 publications, and held no less than 794 Anti-Church Lectures: from 1875 to 1879, inclusive, these Lectures amounted to 4,281), but the statements to be found in the Literature or uttered by the Lecturers are either false or misleading. A line of Juvenal may describe the utterances of the Lecturers—

" Immensa cavi spirant mendacia folles."
Juv: 7, iii.

Still these *mendacia* have their weight with those who know nothing or little about the matter.

Well, how is this ramified organisation to be counteracted, and how are all these false or misleading statements to be met?

Individual Clergy may do much—I do not indeed wish
to recall the days when Pulpits were "tuned" to a certain
note, and I want no personal denunciations of adversaries or
exposure of adverse systems or religionisms or tactics to
advance them, in a place where higher topics and a less
irritant tone should be found to prevail. But surely the
Clergy might take more frequent occasion than they do to
tell their people why they are Churchmen, what is the
pedigree of their Church, how it became, and in what sense
it became, established—and how it is what it is because their
fathers set them examples of that liberality and piety, in
endowing and building churches, which they themselves are
every day so nobly imitating. It is astonishing how much
ignorance prevails upon these important points, even among
the better educated people, and if among them, among
Farmers and Shopkeepers, Labourers and Mechanics. Hence
they are the prey of ill-intentioned agitators—who wishing to
destroy or impair every thing that is venerable and ancient,
choose naturally enough, as their first object of attack, that
which their hearers are least theoretically able to defend.
Church principles are not too abstruse for the general
comprehension, if trouble is taken in inculcating them. And
it is notorious that the Laity, when they have once mastered
them, are more tenacious of them, and more courageous in
asserting them, than the Clergy themselves. A lesson might,
with advantage be gained from the Roman Catholics and the
Nonconformists, who have reasons, such as they are, put
into their mouths for standing aloof from us. Surely the
Clergy should practise analogous teaching. And surely, also,
they need be restrained by no delicacy in pointing to the
Church in each place as the centre of religious affection,
and to the Parsonage as the abode of a kindly heart,
and the fountain of kindly ministrations. And, if Lecturers
come down as emissaries poisoning the minds of their
flock, and meetings are held, and publications are issued

27

of a baneful tendency, these Lecturers might be opposed face to face, the cut-and-dried Anti-Church Resolutions, which have been prepared, replaced by triumphant assertions of the truth against the falsehoods exposed, and these publications confuted by other publications setting forth what is the real state of the case. And a band of Laymen, organised into a Committee, might be easily formed to aid a Clergyman whose heart was really in the enterprise.

But a Clergyman may say, I have not the specific information at hand,—and I am not able to provide any well-disposed Laymen with controversial statements or the materials by which these *mendacia* may be met,—or, I am not able to debate in public, or summon up and marshal my thoughts and information.

A reply is at once ready.

An Institution exists which can (or rather could, for its efficiency must depend in a great measure upon what you choose to do for it,) supply all the aid, both personal and literary, which you can require. It is that to which I have already alluded, "The Church Defence Institution."* Its object is to diffuse sound information on Church questions amongst all classes of people—by the instrumentality of Archidiaconal, Ruri-decanal and Town Branches, and, if necessary, even Parochial Branches. This it would effect by means of organising Secretaries and competent Lecturers in each Province, and by publications specially written and designed to meet vulgar errors and the unfounded assertions of the Liberation Society. I will just show you how it works by some instances. A Rural Deanery in my own Archdeaconry wanted information as to the tactics of the Liberation Society. The Clergy and Laity were to meet in Conference. They sent to Dr. Alfred T. Lee, the Secretary.

---

* Its Office is St. Stephen's Palace Chambers, 9, Bridge Street, Westminster, *S. W.*, and its Secretary, the Rev. Dr. Alfred T. Lee.

The result was the immediate formation of a Branch Church Defence Institution.

Here are some extracts from a few out of many letters of a similar character, which, I understand, have been received at the office of the Institution during the last few months :—

The first comes from an Incumbent in the North.—"We are all delighted with your Lecturer. Our opponents think him very clever and very courteous. We must form a Branch Church Defence Institution in this district,—an old Parish sub-divided into four or five Ecclesiastical Districts. I will subscribe a guinea a year, and as soon as we can organise, will send you all subscriptions I can get. Kindly forward me all plans for Organisation and the Liberation Society's scheme."

The next from an Incumbent in Cornwall.—"I beg to enclose a P.O. order for a subscription to the Institution, which is but a small token of my gratitude for your help, and of my appreciation of the value of the work you are doing. If you could add to your work the employment of an able and well-read Lecturer to refute such Liberation Agents as Mr. ———, who is a very skilful and ready debater, you will add to the debt of gratitude due from Churchmen to you."

The next from a Vicar in Yorkshire.—"As your Agent lectured for us in defence of the Church, I think it only proper to write and say how pleased we were with his Lecture, and that we consider it to have been most useful—it was so thoroughly convincing. The Independent Minister seconded the vote of thanks, and was evidently not in any way aggrieved with what had been said, while he could not in any way gainsay the Lecturer's position."

The next from a Town in Montgomeryshire.—"I thank you most kindly for sending me the leaflets of the Church Defence Institution, and I am glad to inform you that through their aid we won the debate I told you of by 20 to 10."

The next from a Working Man in the West.—" As I am only a working man, (compositor by trade), I am afraid I can do little. I never hear a remark made, derogatory to the Church, doctrinal or otherwise, without challenging it ; and with the aid of your admirable pamphlets, I hope to do more."

A Layman in the neighbourhood of Blackheath reports, " That at a debate held in the Congregational Chapel there, but open to the public, and at which the Treasurer of the Liberation Society presided, a resolution in favour of Disestablishment was lost by 22 votes to 19. This result he attributes to the distribution of papers forwarded by the Church Defence Institution, and to the materials supplied to him and others for their speeches."

And here is an *Extract from a Letter of a Country Archdeacon* who had written to Dr. Alfred T. Lee for a Lecturer, to go down to a meeting in a place which we will call B—, in order to counteract the efforts of Liberationists. It was addressed to the Assistant Secretary of the Church Defence Institution.

" A full description of the meeting at B——— I received last Sunday from a railway porter who spent his Sunday here with my servants—an excellent Churchman, who had been present. He lives in B———, and he says the effect on the place has been marvellous, and just what you and I hoped and anticipated might be the result of your visiting the populations of our small towns and large villages."

The Institution has in circulation a vast number of pamphlets and leaflets, which it is ready to place, at the smallest possible cost and even gratuitously, in the hands of those who desire information on the points with regard to which the Church has been misrepresented.*

* I am glad to say that the Society for Promoting Christian Knowledge has taken up the cause of Church Defence, as indeed it well becomes it to do. "The Englishman's Brief on behalf of his National Church," is one of the most valuable summaries with which I am acquainted, both of objections to the Church as an Establishment, and of the crushing answers which may be given to them. It has many other useful publications of a similar character.

It has also a useful monthly publication, entitled *The National Church*, in which may be found all sorts of intelligence regarding not merely the Church's enemies, but the Church's vigorous friends.

Considering its resources the Institution has already done much. But its income is only some £3,000 or £4,000 per annum, and this to meet the Liberation Society's income of £14,000 per annum. And it cannot adequately carry out its designs without further resources, which I am sure the Church could and ought to supply. I gather from its prospectus that,

I. In the Southern Province (Canterbury) it requires:
    Two organising Secretaries, and
    Two competent Lecturers.

But that, of these, the Institution has at present one organising Secretary, but no salaried Lecturer. Occasional lectures are given from time to time.

II. In the Northern Province, York) it requires:
    One organising Secretary, and
    Three competent Lecturers.

But that, of these, the Institution has one excellent Lecturer by whom a series of Lectures is given in the North throughout the year, but no organising Secretary.

The same document states that constant applications are made for grants of the publications of the Institution, which it is only enabled most inadequately to supply.

And that a number of Debating Societies and Miniature Parliaments exist throughout the country, in which the Church and State question is constantly discussed. A large supply of sound publications on such occasions would be of great benefit; but at present only a meagre parcel can be forwarded.

It rests with you, my Brethren, to provide what is lacking by your influence, your subscriptions, and by your organisation. He who does not resist sacrilege, when he can, makes himself, in some sense, a partaker in its guilt. He who hears a lie, and does not do his part to confute it, aids in the mischief caused by its circulation. The sum specially subscribed for the purposes of the Liberation Society, and its annual income, large as they appear to be, are nothing compared with what Church people could contribute by a general and generous resolve. And it is a notorious fact that the special sum was subscribed, not by many, but by a few opulent Anti-Church people. The Question before us is not a Clerical one merely. For were the Clergy dispossessed to-morrow they would receive some pension. It is a Lay Question also— for though Towns perhaps might find ministrations, Country places would be left to heresy or positive heathenism. Nay, rather it is a question for Clergy and Laity combined. They must consult, they must be brought nearer each to each than they are at present—they must concentrate their energies—in a word, they must thoroughly understand each other. It is from a conviction of the necessity of such mutual understanding that I have witnessed with satisfaction the establishment of Diocesan Conferences, and, as you know well, have pressed the establishment of such a Conference in the Diocese of London, to which I look forward hopefully. Already a vast number of interesting subjects have been treated of at those Conferences. But, so far as I am aware, they have not, with the exception of those of Oxford, Bangor, Ely, Oxford and Winchester,* devoted themselves directly to

---

* The following are all the efforts on the subject which appear in the Reports of the Diocesan Conferences Committee to the Lower House of Canterbury:—

CHURCH AND STATE.

| Oxford | ... 1877 ... | Severance of above highly detrimental to the best interests of the Nation and Spiritual welfare of the Church, and much to be deprecated. |
| Bangor | ... 1875 ... | Most effective manner of meeting the attacks of the Liberation Society in our several parishes. |

the subject of Church Defence. Even in those cases little
or no action seems to have ensued on the Discussions
held, or Resolutions arrived at. This cannot be attribu-
table to indifference. It is rather the result of ignorance
of the extent of the machinations of the Church's enemies,
or of the prevalence of the feeling deprecated, as we have
seen already, in strong terms at the Lambeth Meeting.
' Besides,' good easy people are apt to say, ' Threatened
' corporations and threatened folks live long. A solemn
' decision of the House of Lords was once called by an
' impatient Statesman, "the whisper of a faction," but the
' House of Lords survives, and is likely to survive that and
' more grievous assaults. It is nearly fifty years ago, since
' Earl Grey apologized in the House of Lords for using the
' word " Monarchy " of the chief power, in a free country.
' Yet the Monarchy still exists. And about the same time,
' the same noble Earl advised the Bishops " to set their houses
' in order." Yet Episcopacy still exists, and not merely is
' this the case, but three new Bishoprics have been formed,
' three others are in course of formation, and many other signs
' of life are manifesting themselves in the Church on every
' hand. Church Restoration and Church Extension (in-
' cluding munificent Endowments as well as Building) have

Ely	... 1872 ...	Resolution in favour of Church Defence Associations.
Oxford	1876 ...	The avowed principles of the Church Defence Institution deserve cordial support.

ATTACKS ON CHURCH PROPERTY.

Winchester	... 1878 ...	That attacks on the position and property of the Church of England be resisted.

I have no returns as to this matter from the Province of York. Its
Convocation has not yet tabulated the Resolutions or other proceedings of its
several Diocesan Conferences. But a Committee has just been appointed for
this purpose.

' been largely carried on lately.* These things make it
' difficult to believe that any attack upon the Church can be
' seriously ventured upon. Fifty years ago, Non-conformists
' clamoured for Disestablishment, because the Church was
' *not adequately performing* her functions. Can it be that any
' honest men are clamouring for Disestablishment now, when
' she is *performing* her functions?' Such is the language of
many worthy but not far-seeing persons.

But further, the apathy of which I complain may be—I
believe it is—in a great measure due to the facts that Diocesan
Conferences are not as yet universal, and that even if they
were, no plan exists for directing all of them to simultaneous
consideration of the same matters. It is to be hoped that the
Pastoral which it is understood is about to be issued by the
Archbishop of Canterbury may supply this want—or, if not,
that the organisation of a Central Committee, composed of
deputies from all the Conferences at present formed, will do
something in the desired direction. The nature of such a
Central Committee and of the functions to be assigned to it
is shown in the following important Resolutions passed by the
Conference of Norwich last year :—

" 1. *That a Memorial be presented from this Conference to
the Archbishops and Bishop of the Provinces of Canterbury
and York, desiring simultaneous discussion in the Diocesan
Conferences and Synods of England and Wales, of subjects of
general and pressing importance, and for concerted action in
matters affecting the interests and efficiency of the Church at
large, or her relations with Parliament and Convocation.*

" 2. *That the Synods and Conferences of England and*

---

* It has been stated, and, I believe, correctly, that "since 1818, when
modern Church building may be said to have commenced, no less than 3,015
new Districts or Parishes have been formed, and this represents in round
numbers the Churches which have been built during that period. This
means nearly one Church a week."—*Free and Open Church Advocate.* The
above statement takes no account of Church Restoration which has been well
nigh universal.

Wales be requested to concur in the above Memorial, and to co-operate in establishing a Central Committee, to propose questions for simultaneous discussion, and generally to be the organ of inter-communication and joint action. The Central Committee to consist of the Secretaries of the several Diocesan Synods and Conferences, and two elected Members (one Clergyman and one Layman) from each Synod or Conference."

Among other advantages, the carrying out these Resolutions would bring the Two Provinces of Canterbury and York together, so far as action goes, and obviate the inconveniences produced by two Convocations. I may add that in view of their general adoption, Representatives to serve upon such a Central Committee have been already nominated by the Dioceses of Winchester, Bath and Wells, Chichester, Ely, Lichfield, St. Albans, St. Asaph, and Truro, in the Southern—and by those of Carlisle, Chester, Manchester, and Ripon, in the Northern Province.

It may, perhaps, take some time to bring this about. But it need take no time for individual Churchmen to contribute liberally towards the funds of the Church Defence Institution, which is doing their work already, so far as its means allow. The danger is urgent. Let us not be lulled into security by the comparative rareness of the cry for Disestablishment at the recent elections. We may depend upon it that the storm is gathering certainly, though, for the moment, silently. Pity that we should be taken,

" Regardless of the sweeping whirlwind's sway
That hushed in grim repose, expects his evening prey ! "*

I have detained you longer than I desired upon this important subject. I will only say, before I quit it—do not think that I am an alarmist, in a bad sense, or deficient in Charity, or unregardful that Prayer is our main defence after all. If only a tenth of what I have said is correct, it is

* Gray's *Bard*.

criminal for those who are in anything like a responsible position not to sound an alarm. When the designs of an enemy are manifest both in deeds and in words, to ignore them is not Charity but Fatuity. And I have yet to learn that Prayer and Precaution are incompatible; or that to sit still with folded hands is an essential of faithful Prayer. Such an attitude may become the Mahometan Fatalist, as he indolently murmurs, "It is the will of Allah." It cannot become the Christian.

And yet once more. Do not think that I confound for a moment those two very distinct ideas—the Church as a Spiritual body, and the Church established in a kingdom as a great and visible Corporation. I urge that by maintaining it in its latter aspect, we have found by experience that there are greater opportunities of evangelising our population than would exist if we permitted Disestablishment. And I venture to submit that we are no more justified in throwing these opportunities away, than an individual man would be in neglecting his physical health, because he supposes himself to be occupied with the exclusive care of his soul. A lamented friend of mine once said, "You have but one body to wear out. Why should you not make it last as long as you can?"

But before I conclude, I must, as my custom has hitherto been, advert briefly to certain other topics which concern the framework and material interests of the Church. Some of them I have touched upon in former years, but some of them are new.

The *Burials Bill* is now an Act of Parliament.* We may regret that it has become so, but it will be our true policy to meet it with cheerfulness, just as we are meeting the establishment of School Boards, and the intrusion, in many

---

* Another Act was passed on the 17th of February last, for *the Removal of Doubts concerning the Burial and Registration Acts.*

cases, an unwarrantable one, of Board Schools into our Parishes or their immediate neighbourhoods. In the latter case, we are, if we are wise, keeping up our Church Daily Schools as long as we can, and when this is found no longer possible, making the best terms for their surrender, and securing a paramount influence in the School Boards, besides throwing our energies into our Sunday Schools. So here. Let us abstain from starting frivolous objections or initiating obstacles to the working of the Act.

With regard, however, to the *Education Acts*, though I counsel that the best should be made of them as long as they last, I cannot help thinking that the day must come when their unfairness to the Church and to all sects who prefer their own religious teaching to colourless or non-religious teaching will be more thoroughly recognised than it is at present. It is stated, and I believe accurately, that accommodation is now afforded in Church of England Schools for no less than 2,327,379 children—that is, for about 400,000 more than is afforded by the Board, Wesleyan, Roman Catholic, and other Dissenting Schools put together. The School Board System is not as yet extended over the whole kingdom. But if it were, and if the Church of England and the Denominationalists who care for their own Creeds were put on one side, and thus taxed doubly for their conscientiousness—while on the other those of less yielding conscience were taxed only once, the equity of a General School Fund, such as exists in Lower Canada, would be made manifest. The principle of that Fund is that while every parent would be allowed to choose his School, every School would receive part of the Fund, and thus no person would be taxed more than once. I spoke of this matter, you will recollect, in my Charge of 1876.*

---

* A good deal might be said upon the economy of our Parochial Schools, the expenditure upon which is carefully weighed, as contrasted with the profuse outlay which School Boards enter upon. But I prefer to adduce a

A *Bill for Legalizing,* what is called, *Marriage with a Deceased Wife's Sister,* has been reintroduced. Let us oppose this still, for the many reasons which I have brought before you both in my Charges of 1876 and 1880.

In this respect I indeed deprecate any change in the Laws of Marriage. But they require, as I stated last year, careful revision in other matters. In none of them, however, is revision more urgently required than in the direction which was indicated at a Meeting held on April 6th, last past, at the house of Lord Shaftesbury. I copy a report of it which may perhaps have escaped your notice. The Meeting was held in order to receive an account of a benevolent lady, named Leigh, of her Mission in Paris.

The report says:—

" Miss Leigh dwelt at some length on the French Law of Marriage, and its results to many Englishwomen. She

---

letter from one of the Clergy of the Archdeaconry, which appeared in the *Times,* last February. He wrote thus to the Editor:—

"Sir,—A local example will well illustrate your article of to-day respecting the expenditure of the London School Board on sites and buildings.

"The last Board School was opened a fortnight ago in Amberley-road, Harrow-road. Within five minutes' walk of these Schools are the St. Peter's National Schools, which have been built within the last nine years, and three years ago were almost doubled in accommodation. Her Majesty's Inspector thus reported on the enlargement in September, 1878—'The new schoolroom is an admirable one ;' and, in 1879, ' The teachers have every advantage so far as premises are concerned.'

"Allow me to append a comparative statement of the extent and cost of these two Schools:—

	"St. Peter's School.	Amberley-road Board School.
"Extent of site ...	24,210 sq. ft.	22,000 sq. ft.
"Number of school places provided	757	603
"Total cost	£4,432	£19,586
"Cost per place ...	£5 17s.	£32 9s. 6d.

"I will only add that I have taken into account the gift of sites, &c., of St. Peter's School at their estimated value as presented to the Education Department, and I leave the figures to speak for themselves.

"I am, Sir, your obedient servant,

"W. H. O'BRYEN HODGE, Vicar of St. Peter's,

"February 19, 1881." "Paddington.

repeated the warnings she had previously given in the *Times*, and elsewhere, with regard to the non-recognition by the French Law of Marriages between a Frenchman and an Englishwoman in England contracted in accordance with the English law, and she mentioned some painful cases in which French Communists who had married Englishwomen in London had, after returning to Paris, repudiated their English wives and treated them with the greatest cruelty.

Lord Shaftesbury said that "as to the French law he saw no hope of improvement, the French people being apparently as much attached to their Marriage Law as the Scotch were to theirs. The only thing that could be done was to make it as widely known as possible that if an Englishwoman contracted marriage in England with a Frenchman, in accordance with the laws of this country, and afterwards went to live in France, the marriage could there be dissolved. The evil was a crying one, but he saw no other remedy."

This is good advice for the present, but I trust some other remedy may be found, if with our other representations as to the need of amendment in the Marriage Laws, we press this sad treatment of our young Countrywomen and fellow Churchwomen on the notice of our Government.

I may mention that I have every now and then been consulted by Clergy as to the course which they should take when any marriage is proposed between an English person and a foreigner. I have told them to counsel the parties not to marry without applying for the best legal advice as to the law of the foreigner's nationality that can possibly be procured. I have reason to know that some hazardous ventures have thus been stopped.

Mr. Blennerhasset has *two Bills* before the House of Commons, which are still awaiting a second reading. One is a *Marriage Law Amendment Bill*, to extend the legal hours of marriage, on which Mr. Córbett has given the following notice of amendment:—On second reading of Marriage

Law Amendment Bill, to move " That it is expedient, in the interest of the industrial classes, that facilities should be afforded them for marriage outside working hours, thus avoiding loss of wages; and that it should be rendered obligatory on every Parson, Vicar, Minister, or Curate to solemnise marriages on Saturday from eight o'clock in the forenoon to six o'clock in the afternoon."

The other is a *Marriage Registration Bill*—" To alter and amend the law relating to the Registration of Marriages." And he has also laid the following notice on the Table of the House.

Marriage Law.—" To call attention to the Report of the Royal Commission on the Laws of Marriage, dated 1868, and, in accordance with the recommendations therein contained, to move the following *Resolution:*—' That it is expedient that the law relating to the constitution and proof of the contract of marriage should be simple, certain, and uniform; it should be embodied in a single statute applicable to every portion of the United Kingdom, and such statute should provide that legal marriage must for the future in Scotland, as well as in England and Ireland, always take place in the presence of a duly authorised minister of religion or civil officer.' " It will be our duty to watch carefully the course of the debates on the whole subject. The latter of Mr. Blennerhasset's Bills does not apply to the Church of England, or to Quakers or Jews. But with the former of them, and also with the proposed Resolution, which professes to be based on the Royal Commission, the Church is very nearly concerned.

The Hon. E. Stanhope's *Church Patronage Bill* will, I trust, so far as its main provisions go, pass into a law. Such scandals as have been recently made public as to fraudulent purchases of next Presentations, as to colourable resignations by means of acceptance of Donatives, and as to appointing Clergymen to Livings who are, either from their youth, without experience, or, from their great age, incapable of work, most urgently demand removal. And in order to prevent frauds and simoniacal arrangements, it is absolutely necessary that there should be some authoritative Registration of the Patronage of Benefices, and that the title of no Patron should be admitted, unless his name has appeared in the Registry for a certain time before he prefers a claim to present.

Mr. Monk has a Bill before the House of Commons respecting the *Admission of Churchwardens*. It has been strongly objected to by the Lower House of the Convocation of Canterbury, in the following terms :—

" Mr. Monk's Bill allows any Churchwarden to be admitted to his office by the Incumbent, or the Rural Dean, without attending the Archdeacon's Visitation.

" This will obviously tend to Churchwardens not attending the Visitation, though the Bill no doubt declares that nothing in the Bill is to interfere with such attendance, and precisely the Churchwardens of Parishes (outlying Parishes) which need looking after, will be absent.

" The object of the Bill is expressly to facilitate the admission of Churchwardens, and the effect, no doubt, to avoid Visitation fees. But there is no need of such facilities. Any Churchwarden who cannot conveniently attend the Visitation can go before the neighbouring Surrogate or appear at the Registry. And the Visitation fees are not fees for the admission of the new Churchwardens, but the payment due for the maintenance of the Diocesan Registry—payable by the late Churchwardens, together with other charges for the repair of churches and supply of things required for Divine Service.

" Mr. Monk's Bill, if it became law, would infallibly put an end to the gatherings of Churchwardens, with Clergy, at the Annual Visitations, which are very advantageous in every point of view.

"The individual Churchwarden, in many Archdeaconries, now personally promises the Ordinary (whose officer he is) to present such things and persons as are by law presentable. Under the Bill he will cease to do so, and will soon become the officer of the person who admits him, instead of the officer of the Ordinary. For no sufficient reasons it will introduce a great change, which may seriously affect the relations between the Archdeacon and the Churchwardens, as well in the case of the Churches as in matters of discipline."

Mr. Monk has issued a reply in which he says:—

"Mr. Monk's Bill provides facilities for the admission of Churchwardens by the Rural Dean or the Incumbent—who may be to be considered Surrogates *ad hoc*—so that they may acquire their legal *status* at once, without waiting for the Visitation, which is sometimes postponed for several months.

"It is the undoubted duty of the Churchwardens to attend the Archdeacon's and the Bishop's Visitations, and to make their presentments according to law.

"There is a need for such a measure. No fee can be legally exacted from a Churchwarden for his admission. But when the Visitation is delayed, the Churchwarden can only be admitted by Commission, or by attendance at the Diocesan Registry, and consequently incurs the payment of a fee to the Registrar.

"Though the Churchwarden is a temporal as well as an ecclesiastical officer, Mr. Monk's Bill expressly restricts the power of admission to an ecclesiastical officer, who is empowered to act as a Surrogate *ad hoc*.

"If a Churchwarden determines to neglect his duties and not to attend Visitations, it is not probable that he will be induced to change his mind by a refusal to grant him facilities for his admission to office. The gathering of Churchwardens with Clergy is undoubtedly advantageous to both parties; but it will not be rendered less agreeable by the action of Mr. Monk's Bill, if it becomes law.

"The Rural Dean and Incumbent are as much the officers of the Bishop as are the Archdeacon, Chancellor, and Surrogate."

Out of justice I have laid this reply before you, but I think it hardly meets the points objected to. Therefore, though I am sorry to object to a Bill brought in by a good Churchman, like Mr. Monk, I must adhere to the opinion of the Lower House of Convocation. I conceive that the grievance which the Bill professes to remedy is infinitesimal, that every reasonable facility is already afforded for the admission of Churchwardens who are unable to attend Visitations personally, that the fees spoken of have nothing to do with their admission, but are connected with the Visitation, that their proposed admission by their own Clergyman, whose conduct they may have occasion to present the next year, places them in a false position towards him; and, generally, that the Bill is calculated to impair the very relations which we have long been desirous of strengthening, which bind together the Laity, (through the Churchwardens representing them,) the Archdeacon and the Bishop.

As for postponement of Visitations, this is of comparatively rare occurrence. They generally take place very soon after the usual time of the appointment of Churchwarden. And if there is any urgent cause for early admission to office, the Archdeacon himself, or his official Principal or Registrar in this Diocese, or, in other Dioceses, the Archdeacon's Surrogate, can act in the matter and would act.

I will not detain you by any remarks upon Colonel Barnes' *Corn Returns Bill*, or that of the Hon. E. Ashley on the same subject, (called *Corn Returns Bill No. 2*). As to this latter, the Hon. Wilbraham Egerton will move, on the second reading :—

"That any partial readjustment of the corn averages

under the Act 6 & 7 Will. iv, c. 71, is inexpedient, and that it be referred to a Select Committee to inquire what changes have taken place since the Act of 1836, which may render advisable some modification of the existing law, without any interference with the general principles of that Act."

After its second reading, if it passes that stage, Mr. J. G. Talbot will move that it be referred to a Select Committee. Mr. Inderwick has a Bill waiting a second reading called *The Tithe Extraordinary Charge Bill*, and also a *Motion*, the terms of which seem to be very suspicious. It proposes to appoint a Select Committee with a very broad scope indeed, " To enquire as to the expediency of abolishing extraordinary Tithe Rent-Charges, and providing a scheme for their redemption upon equitable terms ; also to inquire into the present mode of assessing ordinary Tithe, and to report whether any, and what, improvements may be made in such assessment ; and also to inquire into and report upon the expediency of providing greater facilities for the redemption of ordinary Tithes upon equitable terms."

It may be questioned whether any of these proposals will produce immediate action. And it is, perhaps, as well to wait the issue of the Debates to be held upon them. The prevalence of agricultural embarrassment has no doubt promoted their origination at the present time.

The whole subject of Tithes is before a Committee of the Lower House of the Convocation of Canterbury. And I trust that the following alarming fact will not be overlooked by that Committee. On Tuesday, May 3, a Resolution passed the House of Commons in these terms :—

" Resolved, That, in the opinion of this House, it is desirable to abolish the power of levying Distress for the Rent of Agricultural Holdings in England, Wales, and Ireland."

Well, what have the Clergy to do with this? you may say. I reply, A great deal. It is true that a Bill would be required to carry it into effect, but the Government have promised to bring in such a Bill. And it would operate most disastrously upon the Clergy in this way. Under the term *Rent for Agricultural Holdings* may possibly be included *Tithe Rent-charges*. Now by the arrangements of the *Tithe Commutation Act* all personal liability to pay Tithe or Rent-charge is abolished. The remedy provided, in case of non-payment is, after twenty-one days' notice, a right to distrain " in the same manner as Landlords are by law able to distrain for rents in arrear, on yearly or other tenancies," or words to that effect. If then the power of Distraint ceases, how is the Tithe-owner to recover? I do not suppose that this difficulty was thought of, or that the intention of the Resolution was such as it appears to be. But at first sight it seems to suggest a very simple mode of Disendowment. Therefore any Bill which may be founded upon it will require to be watched.

I have advocated on former occasions the establishment of Church Councils in a Parish. I advocate it still.

It is the first link in the chain of communication of their respective views between Clergy and Laity, of which Ruri-decanal Conferences, Diocesan Conferences, and, what I have said already has been also proposed, a Central Committee composed of deputies from all the Diocesan Conferences, are further links. I repeat, I advocate it still. But I must strongly protest against any such spurious management of Church matters as is proposed by Mr. Albert Grey's *Church Boards Bill*. It provides for the election by the Parishioners, if they choose to adopt the Bill, of a Board of persons of which the Incumbent and Churchwardens are indeed *ex officio* members, but the elected members of which need not be members of the Church of England.* The powers of this

---

* A Bill was introduced to legalise Parochial Church Councils (which at present are merely voluntary arrangements), by Lord Sandon, some years ago (in 1871), which passed a second reading. But it differed from that of Mr. Albert Grey in many important points, and especially in its providing that elected members should belong to the Church of England.

Board are to be most extraordinary, and would subject the concerns of the Church to a set of men who might not have the slightest sympathy with her doctrines or spirit. These are clauses 10, 11, and 12:—

" 10. The Board shall have the power from time to time of making any change not contrary to law in the manner of conducting the services and ministrations of the Church, or in the vestments worn by any person officiating or assisting in such services, or in the arrangements for the seating of the Parishioners, or in the lights, ornaments, decorations, furniture, or fittings, of the Church. The Board shall also superintend the distribution of all moneys collected within the Church, and undertake the management of any matter of an ecclesiastical nature affecting the general interests of the Parish, which has theretofore been managed by the Incumbent, or by the Incumbent and the Churchwardens. The Board shall be a body corporate, and shall have power to acquire and hold property of any kind in trust to retain or apply the same for any religious or charitable object connected with the Parish.

" 11. In any Parish in which a Church Board is for the time being established no change shall be made, without the sanction of such Board, in the manner of conducting the services and ministrations of the Church, or in the vestments worn by any person officiating or assisting in such services, or in the arrangements for the seating of the Parishioners, or in the lights, ornaments, decorations, furniture, or fittings of the Church, unless the existing practice which shall be so changed is unlawful.

" 12. Subject to the power of appeal hereinafter contained the Incumbent and Churchwardens shall respectively conform to all lawful orders made by the Church Board under this Act."

An appeal on the part of the Incumbent is indeed allowed in clause 14 to the Bishop, but I think that as the

Church Laity would be very ill-advised if they allowed the Bill to pass, so, the Bishops would find it a very hard task to quiet matters in a Parish where they felt bound in equity to support the Incumbent, or to abet the Church Laity whose feelings were outraged by the acts of such a Board. And as for the Incumbent himself, his condition in reference to it would be by many degrees worse than that of a Minister of the Kirk of Scotland, or of a Dissenting Teacher to their respective Elderhoods or Congregations.

It may be said, perhaps, that there can be no objection to the proposed Board, because the electors will be the same as those who now elect the People's Churchwarden. It should, however, be remembered that the office of Churchwarden, as Lord Stowell has declared, is " an office of observation and complaint, but not of *control*, with respect to Divine worship ;" that is, so far as the Minister is concerned.—(*See* Burn's *Ecclesiastical Law*, by Sir Robert Phillimore, D. C. L., Vol., i. p. 399.) Among their duties are the following :—To take care that order be preserved in the Church and Church-yard during Divine Service ; to watch over the due observance of the Lord's Day in their respective Parishes; to present at Visitation such persons and things as are by law presentable ; to see that the Church, the Churchyard, and fences, be kept in proper order and repair ; to provide the Sacramental bread and wine ; to take the custody of the Church goods ; and to provide, repair, and renew, as often as there may be occasion, all things which are requisite for the decent performance of Divine Service. They are also to call Vestry Meetings for the making of a Church Rate, and for such other Parish business as requires to be submitted to a Vestry ; and at the expiration of their year of office, to render an Account of the sums by them received and expended, to get the same passed by the Vestry, and to transfer the books and balance of moneys to their successors. But they have no power to interfere with the performance of Divine Service, or with the hours thereof ; or with the proper use of the goods and ornaments of the Church ; on all these matters they should refer to the Ordinary. There are all sorts of powers allowed to this Board, and what likeness there is in the constitution of it to the constitution of existing voluntary Parochial Councils which consist strictly of members of the Church I cannot discover.

The second reading of Mr. Albert Grey's Bill was proposed on Wednesday, April 27th, but the time of adjournment arrived before the debate upon it could be concluded, or any division taken. This gives us time for further consideration of its tendency.

I deeply regret, my dear Brethren, that I should have been obliged to speak so long upon matters which are connected mainly with the external condition of the Church. My excuse, however, if one be needed, will be found in the fact that it is the direct and definite duty of the Archdeacon to advise the Clergy on whatever temporal circumstances may affect their influence with their Parishioners. Often, indeed, it is his delight and privilege to step aside, and give them counsel not merely collectively but individually, either on their method of preaching Christ crucified, or on difficulties in their personal career. I am thankful to say that so complete has been the mutual sympathy of you and myself —that such occasions of intercourse have been far from infrequent. And I look back with gratitude upon much kindness and consideration that I have received. One circumstance in particular has occurred during the past year. You will remember that in my last Charge I brought before you the condition of the East of London, and suggested that perhaps you would help me in gathering a Fund to provide the Bishop of Bedford with two Missionary Chaplains for two years, at the modest stipend of £200 per annum each. In full hope that I should obtain the £800 required I issued in July last, to the Incumbents of some of the more opulent Parishes in the Archdeaconry, a Circular which I also put into the hands of private friends. The result has been most cheering and satisfactory. Clergy placed their pulpits at the disposal either of the Bishop of Bedford or of myself—and the proceeds of our appeals were to be devoted to this special purpose. In some cases an ordinary Offertory was given. In other cases friends came forward with most liberal Donations—(you will find an account in the Appendix to this Charge). And not merely have £800 been collected, but nearly £1,000,—so that the Bishop is able to offer not £200 but £250 per annum to the earnest and capable men whom he has enlisted in his work of Evangelisation. It should be understood also that this sum is in addition to a very large amount which has been put into his hands for general purposes.

You have thus shown that no conventional or topographical limits confine your benevolent efforts. The East of London is beyond the boundaries of our own Archdeaconry. But it wanted help and you have helped it. Similar problems await our solution nearer home. Circles exist, like those described recently by the Bishop of Manchester, in which, from whatever cause, the Church is far from holding her own. One of these is to be found in the Rural Deanery of St. Pancras. Another in the Rural Deanery of Enfield—I mean that part of it which is included in the Civil Parish of Tottenham. In the former, there are poor Districts, which a too unsparing use of Subdivision has cut off from the Mother Parish, and which are languishing for want of pecuniary aid, and of Missionary appliances. In the latter, the population has been increasing with a rapidity that has set at naught all existing Ministrations and Church organisation. One scarcely knows what steps to take. In the former, there are two Districts without Churches, the Schools are maintained with the utmost difficulty, one of its Churches is, from faults in its original construction, in a state of utter disrepair, and local resources are not to be had. In the latter are wanted Living Agents and Churches. Let us try whether something cannot be done. And, in what we do, let us avoid former mistakes.

1. Let us have Men first, with a Mission Room or Chapel, to work in, and Churches second.

2. Let us not build Churches too large, or assign Districts too large to be manageable.

3. If we build Churches, let us request the Bishop to insist upon a regulation, which used to exist but has now fallen into desuetude, that before Consecration, a Capital Sum should be provided to insure means of Repair of the Fabric. " The Incorporated Church Building Society " (No. 7, Whitehall), which we ought to support more than we do, is always ready to hold such Repair Funds in Trust. And let us also take care that, as it is now very difficult to carry on National Schools in the face of Board Schools, a good Mission Room is provided for a Sunday School as well as for other Parochial purposes. Both "The Incorporated Church Building Society" and " The Society for Promoting Christian Knowledge" will help us in this.

4. Let us act on system; not helping one Parish exclusively, or simply on its own application, but taking the advice of the Rural Dean, the Archdeacon, or the Bishop.

5. Let us take our Laity into full confidence. They furnish Funds, and are interested in knowing, and have a right to know, how they are applied.

I might mention other circles, but these two are enough to make us feel that a great and laborious work is before us. But, though this is so, I would not close with a desponding note. Our forefathers have done much for us; but we must not rest upon what they have done, but go on. We must not be content with conserving what we have, but extend our operations. We have much to bear, and various adversaries to encounter. Let us not murmur at this. Hard as

D

advance and conservation and endurance and conflict are, our Father sees that these things are good for us, either in the abstract, or considering our day. Whether we can see how they are good, or no, He has given them, and the exhortation remains in force, in spite of our ignorance " In every thing give thanks." * Let us bear this thought in our hearts, and exclaim, in the stirring words of a modern Poet :—†

" God be thanked that the dead have left still
   Good undone, for the living to do—
Still some aim for the heart and the will
   And the soul of man to pursue !

God be thanked for the ills that endure,
   With the glory that's yet to be won
From the hearts we may hope yet to cure
   By the deeds yet reserved to be done !

And thank God for the foes that remain,
   If they hearten us, Friends, for the fight ;
And the mercy that grants to man's gain
   Yet a new gain for ever in sight !"

---

* 1 Thess. v. 18.   † Robert, Lord Lytton.

APPENDIX.

The following is an account of the Sums which I have received in answer to an appeal which I made in July last, to the Incumbents of some few of the richer Parishes in the Archdeaconry, and to Private Friends, for aid in providing the Bishop of Bedford with *two Missionary Chaplains*, or, as he calls them, *Chaplain-Curates*, for his work in the East of London.

I desired to ensure stipends of £200 per annum to each for the space of two years. This would have required £800. But the appeal has been so kindly responded to that nearly £1,000 has been raised, which will enable the Bishop to assign the more adequate stipend of £250 per annum to each for that period, without encroachment on his General Fund.

	£	s.	d.	£	s.	d.
Archdeacon of Middlesex (£25 for two years) ...				50	0	0
Per Archdeacon of Middlesex :—						
The Hon. Wilbraham Egerton, M.P., 23, Portland Gate, Knightsbridge, S.W.... ...	20	0	0			
J. F. Eastwood, Esq., Esher Lodge, Surrey ...	5	5	0			
A Friend	10	10	0			
Charles Churchill, Esq., Weybridge, Surrey ...	50	0	0			
Graham Robertson, Esq., 21, Cleveland Sq., W.	25	0	0			
R. P. Daniell-Bainbridge, Esq., Holly Brake, Chislehurst	3	3	0			
Henry Cazenove, Esq., Lilies, Hardwicke, near Aylesbury	21	0	0			
Rev. Dr. Bellamy, President of St. John's College, Oxford	10	10	0			
J. S. Gilliat, Esq., Charleywood Cedars, Rickmansworth	25	0	0			
James T. Chance, Esq., 51, Prince's Gate, S.W.	20	0	0			
Rev. J. R. Oldham, Ottershaw Vicarage, Surrey	5	5	0			
Rev. Brownlow Maitland, 41, Montague Sq., W.	5	0	0			
J. F. France, Esq., F.S.A., 2, Norfolk Terrace, Bayswater, W....	10	10	0			
Peter Reid, Esq., 30, Norfolk St., Park Lane	10	10	0			
George Chance, Esq., 28, Leinster Gardens, W.	10	0	0			
An Invalid Lady	0	10	6			
Rev. Samuel Kettlewell, 26, Lancaster Gate, W.	5	0	0			
Louis Huth, Esq., 28, Hertford St., Mayfair, W.	10	0	0			
				247	3	6
Carried forward ...				£297	3	6

	£	s.	d.	£	s.	d.
Brought forward ...				297	3	6
Miss Stewart, 5, Cambridge Square, W., per Rev. Cecil Moore				20	0	0
Rev. T. J. Rowsell and Members of the Congregation of St. Stephen's, Paddington (one year) ...				21	0	0
Rev. Dr. Forrest, and Members of the Congregation of St. Jude's, South Kensington, per Major Keith Falconer				20	0	0
St. Mary's, Boltons—Collection in Church of, per Rev. W. H. Du Boulaye				19	3	5
Mrs. Wood, per Rev. W. H. Du Boulaye ...				5	0	0
Rev. G. H. Wilkinson and Churchwardens: Offertory at St. Peter's, Eaton Square (being Subscriptions of £50 for two years)				100	0	0
Hon. and Rev. E. Carr Glyn and Churchwardens: Offertory at St. Mary Abbotts, Kensington ...				53	9	4
Anonymous Member of Congregation of St. Mary Abbotts, per Rev. G. Wingate				1	1	0
Rev. G. F. Prescott and Churchwardens of St. Michael and All Angels, Paddington:—Offertory ...	39	8	0			
Additions to Offertory, per Rev. G. F. Prescott:—						
J. A. Radcliffe, Esq.	10	0	0			
R. H. Hawes, Esq.	10	0	0			
Miss Edith Erskine	2	0	0			
Miss Lyall	1	0	0			
A Lady (Anon.)	0	10	0			
Rev. E. S. Dewick	5	0	0			
Sundry other additions	3	0	0			
				70	18	0
Mr. Welch, of Stoke Newington, towards Chaplains' Stipends, per Bishop of Bedford				5	0	0
Rev. W. Boyd Carpenter and Churchwardens of Christ Church, Lancaster Gate:—Offertory, being Subscriptions of £50 for two years				100	0	0
Rev. Canon Fleming and Churchwardens of St. Michael's, Chester Square:—Offertory, being Subscriptions of £25 for two years, and something over				60	2	4
Rev. Daniel Moore, of Holy Trinity, Paddington ...				5	0	0
Offertory, from Holy Trinity, Paddington, per Rev. Daniel Moore				10	0	0
Rev. Dr. Tremlett and Churchwardens:—Offertory, at St. Stephen's, Belsize Park				88	3	6
N.B.—Annual Subscriptions, included in above:—						
L. A. Tremlett, Parsonage, Belsize Park	1	0	0			
C. Tremlett, ditto	1	0	0			
— Pattison, Esq., 55, Fellows Road	1	0	0			
Carried forward ...				£876	1	1

53

	£	s.	d.	£	s.	d.
Brought forward ...				876	1	1
Rev. Sir Emilius Bayley, Bart., of St. John's, Paddington, out of Funds at his disposal				5	5	0
Rev. J. P. Waldo, St. Stephen's, South Kensington—Collection at Church, *per* Colonel Ravenhill, R.E., Churchwarden				11	10	8
Rev. Dr. Robbins and Churchwardens of St. Peter's, Notting Hill: Offertory				· 20	19	0
Addition to Offertory : Miss Shakespear, 76, Lansdowne Road, Notting Hill				1	0	0
Rev. T. Teignmouth Shore : Offertory, Berkeley Chapel				15	0	0
				£929	15	9
Additional Sums have been promised and are expected, which will raise the Total to				£1,000	0	0

I subjoin to this statement a letter which has been recently issued by the Bishop of Bedford to all the Incumbents under his immediate care. It will, I am sure be interesting to you, for it shows the many useful ways in which he intends to employ the Clergy with whom you have helped me to furnish him.

" Stainforth House,
" Upper Clapton, London, E.
" My dear Brother,   " Easter, 1881.

" By the kind efforts of the Archdeacon of Middlesex, and the liberality of various Congregations appealed to, I am able to employ two Clergymen, of well-proved fitness for the work, as ' Chaplain-Curates,' or Mission Preachers, for general work in East London.

" I think it will probably help you to judge whether they can be of any use in your Parish, if I enumerate the principal ways in which I look forward to their being employed. Will you kindly communicate with them yourself, if you are desirous of availing yourself of their services in any of the ways suggested, or in any other way.

" Believe me ever,
" Your faithful Friend and Brother,
" WM. WALSHAM BEDFORD.
"(*Bishop Suffragan for East London.*)"

CHAPLAIN-CURATES.

The Rev. C. E. T. Roberts, Gothic House, St. Ann's Road, N.
The Rev. H. J. Stephens, 4, Castlewood Road, Clapton Common, N.

SUGGESTED MODES OF EMPLOYMENT.

1.—Occasional Parochial Missions.

2.—Courses of Special Sermons or Addresses in Churches or Mission Rooms.

3.—The Assistance of Clergy in cases of Sickness or other emergency.

4.—Addresses to Men, whenever opportunity can be found.

5.—Work among those engaged in special employments, such as Policemen, Sailors, Cabmen, Dock-labourers, Costermongers, &c.

6.—Very short mid-day Addresses in Factories or Workshops.

7.—Open-air Addresses.

8.—Assistance in the formation and conduct of Bible-Classes on Sundays or Week-day Evenings.

9.—Addresses to Women at Mothers' Meetings, &c.

10.—Addresses to Sunday School Gatherings, whether of Teachers or of Senior Scholars.

11.—Special Addresses on the subject of Confirmation, or to gatherings of former Confirmation Candidates.

12.—Preaching for the East London Church Fund.

The Bishop adds to this, that (as the work in his District requires very special training), Mr. Roberts will take into his house a few young men preparing for Ordination, and desirous of having their first experience of Pastoral Work with titles in East London.

www.ingramcontent.com/pod-product-compliance
Lightning Source LLC
Chambersburg PA
CBHW021639270326
41931CB00008B/1085